Prayers and Poems
From the Heart

Prayers and Poems From the Heart

Reflections for the Glory of His Holiness

Anamarie Lopez

Prayers and Poems From the Heart:
Reflections for the Glory of His Holiness
Copyright © 2019 by Anamarie Lopez

All Scripture references are from *The Holy Bible: English Standard Version*. Wheaton: Standard Bible Society, 2016.

ISBN 10 – 1642541648
ISBN 13 – 9781642541649

Printed in the United States

Dedication

To Dad, Mom, Juan Carlos,
Jenn, James Marcos and Jasmine:
Wonderful gifts from God that
have blessed my life.

Contents

Acknowledgments

I thank God for giving me the freedom to express myself through these written words. I also thank my loving family and friends for their encouragement during this learning process. I want to especially express my deepest gratitude to my papstor (father and pastor) and Dr. Nancy Nethercott, whose encouraging words and editing help made this project a reality.

Preface

This journey started one beautiful sunny day as I looked outside the window next to my desk. As I looked up at the clouds, I began to think of what it will be like when I get to heaven. Because I always loved poetry, I decided to take my thoughts and turn them into a poem. After reading the poem to my mom, she encouraged me to write more and "who knows," she said, "maybe you can a write a book of poems." I thought the idea was crazy. How can a teenager write a book? Nevertheless, my mom and dad encouraged me to use any and all gifts God gave me for His Glory. And there began my mission.

God has used several ways to help me create my poems. Sometimes listening to my papstor (my pa and pastor) and others preach have inspired me. Poems have come to my mind as I sat at church in silence, just looking at the cross behind the baptistery. Also, by looking at nature as we drove to my brother's house. Believe it or not, just listening to adults having conversations has inspired me to write a few poems.

As I began my journey of writing this book, I noticed how important it became in my life. It is important because I want adults to realize that teenagers do in fact reflect on God, His Holiness, and live in awe of His power and majesty. So, through this book, I hope to encourage teenagers to embrace their talents for God's glory.

The words in these poems have helped me find my voice. They have confronted me, and they have helped me look at my life and how I am living it. And while others preach and teach, I pray I can touch someone through my words in print. God is too great to put into words, but I want to praise and honor Him.

I am greatly inspired by the love of my family. I could not have asked for a better family from God. Their support, encouragement, and help are the reason why this book exists. I pray this book will give Glory to God the Father, God the Son, and God the Holy Spirit.

Anamarie Lopez
Fleming Island, FL
August 2017

When I Get to Heaven

For behold, I create new heavens and a new earth,
and the former things shall not be remembered
or come into mind.

Isaiah 65:17

I can't wait to get to Heaven,
Where my Lord lives and reigns,
Where there are angels,
Streets of gold,
And where there is no more pain.

Where my Father has made a castle for me
And where I will see my
Savior's face for the very first time.

But for now I must wait,
Until the Lord calls me home.
I must stay on this Earth fighting
Sin and temptation and going
Through tribulations until I die.

When I get to Heaven,
Like my brothers and sisters in the faith
We will say,
"I have fought the good fight."
That Glorious day,
We will sing
"Holy, Holy, Holy,"
To our Lord, King, and God Almighty.

Reverence

Then he said, "Do not come near; take your sandals off your feet,
for the place on which you are standing is holy ground."

Exodus 3:5

There is a line we all should know.
Not the equator or what we learn at school,
But a line where we leave
The things of the world behind us
And we mentally prepare ourselves to be in
The presence of our Lord:
Reverence.

In biblical times long ago,
It was a veil,
But now it is when we enter
The front doors of our church:
Reverence.

Over the years,
We have become dull
To this important thing,
For all Christians should have this
For it is what the Lord commands:
Reverence.

The Cross

For the word of the cross is folly to those who are perishing,
but to us who are being saved it is the power of God.
1 Corinthians 1:18

The Cross is something very special
That we cannot merely comprehend.
But we wear this around our necks as fashion
Or on our walls as décor.
Oh, Christian, do you truly understand?
That on a tree
 For three hours of Eternity,
The Father was separated from His son.
And instead of rushing down to save Him,
He, the Father,
Poured all His wrath and anger down on His beloved son.
And our Lord without complaint
Drank it all down, not one drop was left,
In the cup of God's wrath.

Oh, Christians, get on your knees
And praise the Lord,
For that Cross that you wear around your neck
Should not be taken so lightly.
For on the third day
He rose again from the grave,
Defeating sin and death,
And gave us hope
And salvation to the elect.
So, don't just wear that Cross,
Go and preach the good news to all.
Don't waste the beautiful blood of Christ.
Go and tell the world
Why you wear the Cross around your neck
And adorn it on your walls.
For the punishment was paid on that gruesome Cross.

Humbleness

It's barely given any thought,
Because of our sinful trains of thought.
We know it from afar
And yet it's not within us.

Oh Christians,
How can you think that you can escape it?
How can the creation be more than its Creator?
The Lord Almighty,
The one who created Heaven and Hell!
Who deserves all Majesty!
Humbled himself to become a simple babe.
Sinners, Humble yourself before him
Repent from your sinning ways
And give the Lord
Exalted praise.

Jesus

He was born in a stable crying,
To later hang on the Cross dying.

He was the perfect human being
We all wish we could be.
Just ask your parents,
Believe me.

He walked on this Earth preaching the Word
For thirty-three years of His eternity.
He fought hypocrites and serpents in tunics,
He walked with His disciples
Of very little faith.
One would betray him
And one Apostle he would blind
In order to spread the news of his Gospel story.

He is now seated at the right hand of His father.
And will forever have the scars
He had to pay
For our sinful ways.

Oh My Savior

Oh Lord, how great you are
You have saved me from Your wrath,
You have called me one of Your own
By this I am taken with awe.

Oh my Savior,
You saved me from the path of destruction.
You have sealed me with Your Holy Spirit.

I, an evil sinner,
Do not deserve Your mercy,
But only Your anger and wrath.
There are no words to describe the joy I feel
That You chose me to be Your child,
From this wicked, sinful, beastly, and spiteful world.
What could I give you?
Only merely dirty and filthy rags.

Oh my Lord and Savior,
But now I can present crowns before Your feet,
Through the beautiful and Holy blood of Your son,
Jesus Christ,
Oh my Savior.

Do You Truly Love God?

*And you shall love the Lord your God
with all your heart and with all your soul
and with all your mind and with all your strength.*
Mark 12:30

God, I love you.
What a risky thing to say.
Do you truly understand what that means?

It is easy to speak from the mouth,
But do your actions reflect what you say?
Do you call sin what is sin?
Is your yes, yes and your no, no?
"If you love me obey my commandments."
"Love your brother as yourself."
Do you do these very things?
Or are you as selfish as can be?
How long have you saddened the Spirit?
Who, with love, gave your testimony.
Do you truly understand what it is to love God?
Have you been threatened with sword or spear?
Or fire to burn or water to drown?

Oh, wretched sinner
You are not worthy to say such a thing.
Everyday you kill with your heart.
You vote for those who are against the very things your faith believes.

Do not be blinded by whether they're male or not.
If you truly love God,
Stand your ground and don't give Satan the victory he yearns.

God will keep His promises to His children.
Are you of his flock or are you here for the ride?
Only His sheep know the pastor's call.
Do you truly love the one true God?

Revive Us

Heal me, O LORD, and I shall be healed;
save me, and I shall be saved,
for you are my praise.
Jeremiah 7:14

Oh my Lord forgive us,
What has happened to Your people?
What has happened to the fire in our hearts?
And the conviction we once had?
What happened to preaching Your Word of repentance?
And not of what the flesh wants to hear or feel.

Give us that passion we once had,
Take away the fear of persecution.
Bring us to our knees and fill our hearts with repentance.

For we have turned the other way.
Stop the church from conforming to this world,
Instead, renewing our minds in You.
Oh my Lord how I beg of You,
Revive us once again.

Give Me Faith

...for we walk by faith, not by sight.
2 Corinthians 5:7

Lord, in this time of need
I ask You to give me faith for Your glory.
That through me they can see
That I am one of Your chosen seed.

Give me the faith of Noah
Who believed in Your Word.
He built and preached like You commanded
And was saved from the waters of destruction.

Give me the faith of Abraham
Who left his home of luxury
To live a life of service to You,
To start a great nation
To bring the Messiah of salvation.

Give me the faith of Mary
Who gave herself to be used to carry
Your Beloved Son.
To bring the Savior into this sinful world,
To bring hope to the lost.

Lord, in this time of need
I ask You to guide me
That they can see Your seed
has been planted in me
For Your Honor and Glory.

Where There is Pain There is Hope

For I consider that the sufferings of this present time
are not worth comparing with the glory
that is to be revealed to us.
Romans 8:18

Where there is pain, there is hope
For those who believe
Beyond this land and sea.
To those who believe, pain is gain
For the Glory of the King.

For all the troubles in this world
Could not compare to what He endured.
To die on the Cross in such a way
Humiliated, for everyone to see.
But there is hope because He lives and reigns
In Glory with all majesty.

Where there is pain, there is hope
For those who believe.
For there is no greater honor
Than to die for the King of Kings.

Psalm 8

O LORD, our Lord,
how majestic is your name in all the earth!
Psalm 8:9

When we stop to think of Your greatness
We look up
We see the dark night and the light of day
that shines in the sky.
Yet, You are mindful of us.
We are lower than angels,
Yet we will have crowns of glory
When You come back in all Your glory.

You let us take care
Of all Your creatures and land
As far as the eye can see.
What great mercy You have shown Your people
You are surely the King of Kings
And the Creator of all living things.

Proverbs 10:4-6, 19

Blessings are on the head of the righteous...
Proverbs 10:6

Lord help me in this day and age
To overcome the temptations that come my way.
Prevent me from being slack of hand,
But give me the diligent hand
Of a strong, hard, working human.

Let me gather the fruit of the harvest
And not cause shame to my name.

Make me just, as You are just
For You send blessings upon Your chosen ones everyday.
Keep me away from the mouth of the wicked
For violence comes from it.

Stop my mouth from sinning
Against your Holy Word and people.
Refrain my lips from being used
By the devil's sneaky ways,
But make me wise, as You are wise for all the rest of my days.

My Creator

*Worthy are you, our Lord and God, to receive glory and honor and power,
for you created all things, and by your will they existed and were created.*

Revelation 4:11

Oh my blessed Creator,
You created the world and the stars
And all things above and below the sea,
And You created me.

You, in Your perfect way,
Knew who I was going to be.
You gave me the talents You wished
And made me the way You saw fit.

So I give You my talents,
Do, as You will.
Let them give You honor and praise.
Crush my pride, if need be
So You can get all the Glory and Majesty.
For You are my Creator
And my talents are worth nothing
If I don't have You, my Lord and Savior.

It's A Privilege

Count it all joy, my brothers, when you meet trials of various kinds,
for you know that the testing of your faith produces steadfastness.
And let steadfastness have its full effect,
that you may be perfect and complete, lacking in nothing.
James 1:2-4

How twisted are our minds today,
That we cannot see the beauty of God's ways.
For the modern Christian, God's ways
Are rocky, painful, and tough.
But it's because they cannot see what's underneath.

It should not be a burden
Or a thorn to our side,
But a privilege to be chosen for such a task.

Suffering is a privilege we should all want to have.
It's not an easy thing, I know.
For if the Master suffered, who are we not to.
For greater is our reward in Heaven;
Not here on Earth which will all one day vanish
Like a summer's breeze in the mist of the night.
How God Almighty has chosen us,
To carry His Word to all people who breathe!

It's a privilege to suffer.
But if you think not, is your pride so high
That the One who created you in the womb
Had to give His life for you?
Repent of that devilish way
And thank the Lord for the tribulation
that is in your way.

For when you suffer you will grow
Closer to the Lord.
Show the world that what we believe in
Is the one True Lord
And God above all.

Joy

Though the fig tree should not blossom,
nor fruit be on the vines,
the produce of the olive fail
and the fields yield no food,
the flock be cut off from the fold
and there be no herd in the stalls,
yet I will rejoice in the LORD;
I will take joy in the God of my salvation.
Habakkuk 3:17-18

Happiness is all we want;
That's what we all say.
But happiness is such a fleeting thing;
It's here today and gone tomorrow.
Anything can take away our happiness
And turn it into sadness.

So don't ask for that silly thing.
Joy is what we want;
Joy will stay with you
Through the eye of the storm and the tempest.
Joy is peace.
Through the valley when everything seems to be crashing down, we have
peace.
But our joy is not in vain.
No, because it's in the One who gave us salvation.
He is our Joy and Peace,
He is our Comforter,
Our Prince of Peace.

How Do You Find Patience?

But if we hope for what we do not see,
we wait for it with patience.
Romans 8:25

Many people have asked for it,
But not many people have it.
It does not come easy;
It takes a lot of work.
That's why it's discarded
And not attempted to be achieved.

Many try yoga or tea,
They will try anything.
But I look to the one thing that can teach me.
The Bible is my guide through everything.
Tribulation…
That's what it takes to have such a thing.
Didn't our Lord suffer?
And go through hard times?
And yet He had patience
Even on the Cross,
making sure everything was finished.

So Lord help me through the tribulations
That I may be more like You
In everything and every day.

Who Do You Trust In?

Trust in the Lord with all your heart,
and do not lean on your own understanding.
In all your ways acknowledge him,
and he will make straight your paths.
Proverbs 3:5-6

Trust is so important to us in this day and age.
If we don't have it
We're like babies without protection.

Who do you trust?
Your parents, of course
Is the first answer you'll say.
Or maybe a friend that you know
That seems to know you better than you know yourself.
But remember they are all sinners
That fall everyday.

Do you put your trust in idols?
They have eyes and can't see;
They have tongues and can't speak;
They have feet and can't walk.
Idols that can be broken into pieces
And be blown away by the wind.

No, I put my trust in the One
Who commands the wind and the sea,
Who created us individually.
He is the Creator of all wonderful things
And in Him I put my trust for all eternity.

Guide Me Lord

Blessed is the man who walks not in the counsel of the wicked, nor stands in the way of sinners, nor sits in the seat of scoffers; but his delight is in the law of the LORD, and on his law he meditates day and night. He is like a tree planted by streams of water that yields its fruit in its season, and its leaf does not wither. In all that he does, he prospers.

Psalm 1:1-3

Dearest Lord,
It's easy to be led astray in our wandering
And follow the path that seems so welcoming,
But it could be condemning.

Lord, help me not to walk in the way of evildoers.
Guide me away from the path of sinners.
Keep me away from doing injustice
For that path leads to death and destruction.

Guide me in Your Word,
To be like a tree
That gives good fruit for Your Glory;
To be filled with Your Spirit
To learn and share Your perfect Word.
Let me prosper doing Your will
And not my own.

Guide me Lord in this life,
Until I am safe in Your arms
For all eternity and for evermore.

False Prophets

Behold, I am against those who prophesy lying dreams, declares the LORD,
and who tell them and lead my people astray by their lies
and their recklessness, when I did not send them or charge them.
So they do not profit this people at all, declares the LORD.
Jeremiah 23:32

To me it is such a pity
To see the flock being led astray
By all these false prophets
Claiming to be God everyday.

Are we not ashamed
Of what they are doing to the Holy Word today?
Causing false hope to the weak,
Making God a joke.
But one day they will burn
In Hell's Lake of Fire
Where they will be in torment
For all eternity.

"Blessed are those who trust in Him,"
Says the Lord.
Stay true to the Lord
Who will have the revenge one day,
On all of those who blasphemed His Name.

My Heart Is Breaking

O LORD my God, I cried to you for help, and you have healed me.

Psalm 30:2

Oh Lord Almighty,
You have all the Glory.
Have mercy on Your people
And on this nation in which I live.

My heart is breaking everyday
When I see Your people being treated in such a way
That I know that You have called them to be yours.
But there are others that when it gets tough
They cower and run the other way.

My heart is breaking for those who say
They are one of Yours, but You can see
It's a lie that they tell themselves.

Let us be faithful to You
When there is no fruit on the trees,
When there is no water in the streams,
And no harvest in the fields.
I will stay true to You.
You are my Strength and Salvation.

Come fix this breaking heart of mine
Until I am kneeling before You
When my time comes
To praise your Holy Name in the heavens
And my heart is healed and made anew.

Oh My Nation

To the Lord our God belong mercy and forgiveness,
for we have rebelled against him and have not obeyed
the voice of the LORD our God by walking in his laws,
which he set before us by his servants the prophets.
Daniel 9:9-10

Oh great nation of mine
What has happened to you?
Your foundations were made
On the biblical truth of God.
And now you have turned to the pagan world,
Where Satan rules and reigns,
Where sin is loved and praised.

Oh great nation, Oh my nation,
I pray for you everyday.
I pray that you leave this pagan way.

Lord, help this nation and all the nations
Where Your faithful ones live.
Give us a faithful leader,
To turn us back to biblical truths once again.

Wake Up

Besides this you know the time,
that the hour has come for you to wake from sleep.
For salvation is nearer to us now than when we first believed.
The night is far gone; the day is at hand.
So then let us cast off the works of darkness
and put on the armor of light.
Romans 13:11-12

It is such a shame
To see my nation's values being thrown away
Because they offend our feelings.

We are so worried of hurting
Someone's feelings
That we will do anything
So that they will not complain.

Wake up you sinners that claim to love Christ.
God came to earth in the flesh,
He did not come to make us feel good
But to give us salvation through grace.
In His Holy Word He gave us values
And told how we need to strive to be more like Him.

So wake up, Christians!
Where is your armor and shield?
Don't let these sinners
Take this nation down to destruction.
We are one Nation Under God.
Not one Nation Under Feelings.

Propose In Your Heart

But Daniel resolved that he would not defile himself...
Daniel 1:8

It is easy to be led astray
By the desires of the flesh
Every single day.

We must pray for our faith to be strengthened
And our values and convictions
In Christ to grow more and more everyday.

We must not let sin be part of our values and convictions
Or we will fall into a hole from which we can't come out.
If God doesn't tolerate one sin
We shouldn't tolerate it either.

Let us be like Daniel
And propose in our hearts
To follow God's rules and values.
Let us also take action to do it everyday.
Then we will say,
"For me and my house we will serve the Lord,"
Until the end of our days.

Persecution

Look all around you
It's nothing new.
It's been around from
Before you were born until this very moment.

Christians these days fear this thing,
They believe it's never going to come,
Until it knocks on their front door.

Look all around you
Turn on your TV's
It was foretold in the Gospels,
Why has it taken you by surprise?

What will you do when that time comes?
Will you cower and reject the Name of God?
Will you stand like a mighty army and preach the word?
What will you do when you are persecuted in Jerusalem?
Will you stay with your people and die in Babylon?
Or run away to the pagan world and fall to destruction?
What will you do?

Help This Great Nation

Blessed is the nation whose God is the LORD,
the people whom he has chosen as his heritage!
Psalm 33:12

Lord, protect us in this time of need
When everything seems
To be spiraling down to the depths of the sea.

We were once a great nation
That looked to You for everything
Now we look on You as nothing.

Revive us once again,
Let us be quiet no more.
Let us shout Your name from the rooftops
To give You Glory for evermore.

Help this great nation come back to You,
For if You are with us, who can be against us?
Do not leave us in the enemies' hands
Send us a great leader to guide us
Back to Your path once again.

A Godly Man

*Husbands, love your wives, as Christ loved the church
and gave himself up for her, that he might sanctify her,
having cleansed her by the washing of water with the word.*

Ephesians 5:25-26

A Prophet, that is what he must be.
One who preaches God's word
To all human beings.

A Priest, that is what he must be.
To teach and raise my children
In God's word so they can become good Christian sheep.

A Provider, that is what he must be.
To give my children and me
A roof over our heads at night to sleep,
To provide us with food
Not only for our soul
But also for the body that was made for this world below.

A Protector, that is what he must be.
To give protection to our family
From the evil of the world in which we live.
But even before protecting a family,
If he loves me he must be willing
To protect this delicate heart of mine.

I shall wait for you, in God's own time.
Until I can say, "I do"
To you.

True Beauty

*But let your adorning be the hidden person of the heart
with the imperishable beauty of a gentle and quiet spirit,
which in God's sight is very precious.*

1 Peter 3:4

What is true beauty?
Is it what you wear?
Or
What tag is placed on your clothes?

What is true beauty?
Is it how you fix your face?
Or
What type of creams you use
To make your skin all silky smooth?

True beauty
Is not what the world sees
It's what God sees.
And what He sees inside of you
Is what He created
When you were first conceived.
What is that?
You may ask. The answer is one thing:
Your heart.

Marriage

Then the LORD God said,
"It is not good that the man should be alone;
I will make him a helper fit for him."
Genesis 2:18

Love and marriage
Is like a horse and carriage
At least,
That's what they all say.

Marriage is a sacred covenant
That has its up and downs.
That love and marriage
May seem unbalanced like a very large carriage.

Marriage is special and set by God.
And he will help you
With the unbalanced carriage
Until you are with your small carriage
Once again.

Poetry

It's a way to recover
From the stresses of the day.
A way to express yourself
With something so simple as pencil and paper.
With help from the Lord above
You may touch a struggling heart.

Poetry, thus looked at from afar,
No matter how short it may be,
Can be used by the Lord
To save a soul for His Glory.

Children

Behold, children are a heritage from the LORD,
the fruit of the womb a reward.
Psalm 127:3

We were all there once
So small and fragile
Needing the care of a great wise adult.

They sat on His knee
And listened to Him preach.
Jesus loves the little children
No matter where they are from.

Have the faith of a child
And you will inherit the Kingdom of Heaven.
Having the faith of a child
Is a fruit of the truest believer.

Dreams

When the mystery was revealed to Daniel in a vision of the night.
Then Daniel blessed the God of heaven.
Daniel 2:19

When you close your eyes at night
You float away into a place
Where your imagination
Runs wild and free.

Where you can do anything
Where you can rule the largest empire
Known to all humanity.

And just as you've won the hand of your fair maiden
Or
You've danced with your knight in shining armor
You hear a familiar voice
You notice it's the morning calling you from afar.

Your eyes open in amazement,
It seemed so real,
But you realize it was just a dream
From the depths of your imagination.

Christmas

Therefore, the Lord himself will give you a sign.
Behold, the virgin shall conceive and bear a son,
and shall call his name Immanuel.
Isaiah 7:14

The most wonderful time of year
When we all get together
To celebrate one very special thing.

It's not Santa and his reindeers,
Not Frosty the snowman,
But one Man
Who humbled Himself and was born in a stable.

The most wonderful time of year
Is when we all come to celebrate
Our Savior Jesus Christ,
The Lord.

Fathers

My son, do not despise the LORD's discipline or be weary of his reproof,
for the LORD reproves him whom he loves,
as a father the son in whom he delights.
Proverbs 3:11-12

Big, strong, and loving
That's what they are
To those that look up to them.

They are the heroes that fix everything
No matter what it may be.
We know they love us
Even when their discipline is tough.
Tough love,
That's what it takes to form good character for our lives.
So, one day when we're fathers and mothers
We will understand it too.

So, we thank our fathers everyday
For the love they have for us.
Even though one day, as they get older and gray
They will be looking up to us
To be big, strong, and loving
Like the adults they raised us to be.

Mothers

Her children rise up and call her blessed.
Proverbs 31:28

Small, gentle, and sweet
The one that takes care of us
During the day
And at night when we sleep.

They carried us for nine months
Fed us and looked after us
From infancy to adulthood
They were there every step of the way.

They watched us cry and smile,
From our first step to our graduation day.

They calmly taught us lessons
To make us better Christians everyday
So that one day
When we're mothers and fathers ourselves
We can say,
"This is what your grandmother told me when I was your age."

My Wedding Day

All girls dream of it…
Of that very special day
They picture in their minds
Every single day
Just how it may be on their wedding day.

That day for me
I will never stop dreaming of.
When I will be covered in white
From my head to my toes
When that day finally arrives
After all the years of praying, waiting, and wondering
Have all come true.

The day when I can finally say,
"I do" to you,
To my godly man.
When we get together for the joining
Of two people becoming as one.

I know one day
When I am old and gray
I will smile back on that day
As if it was yesterday,
And share it with all my children and grandchildren
And tell them how my dream came true
On that very special day
Called, My Wedding Day.

Music

Praise him with trumpet sound; praise him with lute and harp! Praise him with tambourine and dance; praise him with strings and pipe! Praise him with sounding cymbals; praise him with loud clashing cymbals! Let everything that has breath praise the LORD! Praise the LORD!

Psalm 150:3-6

Notes, notes, so many different notes,
Some go high to the Heaven's sky,
And others go low to the ocean's deeps below,
All created by our Lord.

Notes, notes, so many wonderful notes,
All notes sound beautiful alone,
But together with ties and slurs,
You find it brings music,
Not only to your ears, but to your heart and soul.
The music may make you feel sad or mad,
Even happy and glad.

Music is a musician's offering of gratefulness to God.
The music we will hear
On that marvelous day,
Will be filled with power and majesty,
Joined with voices praising our King for eternity.
Our faces will shine that day
Our hearts and spirits will be filled with a song,
That the universe will hear for all eternity.

The music we will play,
For our God, the King
Will give Glory and Honor to His Name,
Who deserves all Majesty,
Who reigns supreme.

So Let It Be

I have been crucified with Christ.
It is no longer I who live,
but Christ who lives in me.
Galatians 2:20

How can I show love to the One
Who died for me?
Only by surrendering everything.
If this body should be hurt
For He who reigns supreme,
So let it be.

How can I show devotion
To Him who took all the wrath on a tree?
Only by giving Him my all in everything.
Send me into the heat of battle
Send me, Send me
So let it be.

If it be to Death!
So let it be
I'd rather die on Earth
And be with the King in glory
Than to have the world
And burn in Hell with His enemies for all eternity.

God Is Powerful

I don't understand why people doubt God's power every day.
Can't they see God's power in every way?
Through disease, tribulation, or pain
To save a soul that's being led astray.

In the Bible I see God's hand
And power in everything.
In everything there was a purpose
A clear and ordered plan
That not even our mortal minds can comprehend.

When I was younger I knew the story
How Jesus rose from the dead,
But now all I see is the power of that resurrection.
The power that now sin and death have no sting
How that power has brought Salvation
By the Grace of God, to me.

That is all that I need
To know that no false god has died for his sheep.
But the one true God
Has victory and power over all.
Over Demons, Death, and The Devil
He reigns supreme.
With overflowing love and mercy
That rescued me,
From the burning coals of Hell's fire, where Satan will be.

So give thanks to God for His power,
It will never be defeated,
Give glory to God, our King.

Birds

Birds are God's creatures
They come big and small
With Colors that bring enchantment
To the eyes of the beholder.

Birds are God's creatures
That give music to our ears.
Birds are mysterious creatures
That evolution cannot explain.

Birds are God's creatures
So beautiful and mysterious
True works of art
From our Lord above.

Snowflakes

"Come now, let us reason together, says the LORD:
though your sins are like scarlet,
they shall be as white as snow;
though they are red like crimson,
they shall become like wool.
Isaiah 1:18

Gentle and small
With designs no one can see
That fall from the sky
Upon the land and sea.

Soft and cold
When they land on your nose
They can come in a miserable night of Earth's winter below

It's God's way to put a smile on your face
For their beauty you can miss
If your eyes wander off
For your blessing may come
As gentle as a snowflake's kiss.

Trees

*And out of the ground the Lord God made to spring up
every tree that is pleasant to the sight and good for food.*
Genesis 2:9

They stand so big and tall
Straight as a ruler
Can't you see?
That no one taught it how to be.

How to change the colors of its leaves
From season to season
Unless it's an evergreen.

There is only one that can make such a thing
He is the Creator of all living things.
He is bigger, taller, and stronger
Than any tree could ever be.

Flowers

Small and beautiful
That's what we see.
But what is the purpose
Of this living thing?

God created it to give
Oxygen to our lungs
So we could breathe,
To give nectar
To the birds in need.

You see
God creates everything with a purpose
No matter how big or small
It may seem.

Stars

So far away
They light up the night sky,
So perfectly placed
From the beginning of time.

They show us the way
On the land and sea
To where we want to be.

They're too many to count!
Nevertheless, He knows them all by name
From the smallest to the biggest
They are perfectly made
They will shine until the end of days.

Look

The heavens declare the glory of God,
and the sky above proclaims his handiwork.

Psalm 19:1

Look all around you.
What do you see?
Trees!
That's what I see,
Trees of all different kinds.
Some tall, some small
With flowers or fruit
Saying hello to you
As you walk off to school.

Look at the ground.
What do you see?
Grass!
That's what I see,
Collecting the morning dew
To give life to the plants and trees
During night and day
And while we work or play.

Look up at the sky.
What do you see?
Clouds!
That's what I see,
Bringing rain each month and year.
Oh look, birds!
That's what I see,
Dancing in the clouds
Feeling wild and free.

This reminds me of one thing.
How blessed we are to see
Such a beautiful masterpiece
That the lord has made for you and me.

Someone Great and Strong

I am the Alpha and the Omega," says the Lord God,
"who is and who was and who is to come, the Almighty.
Revelation 1:8

What's that sound?
It's like a baby's cry
So small and so fragile,
Susceptible to dangers all around,
Needing the help of someone great and strong.
But there is Someone
Who watches all day long.
He knew you
Before the day you were born.
Trust in Him dear and sweet baby
For He is the King Almighty.

The Importance of Family

And these words that I command you today shall be on your heart. You shall teach them diligently to your children, and shall talk of them when you sit in your house, and when you walk by the way, and when you lie down, and when you rise.

Deuteronomy 6:6-7

We don't think about it today
Because it gets in our way.
We think it's nothing
Not worth our time
But it's more important than you may think.

We have set it aside.
But haven't you noticed
It's what made a nation come alive.
To raise the family in God
Helped this nation to climb to the top.

The importance of family
Is not something fake like a fantasy.
It's the truth, a reality.
The blessing of our freedom
That was given to us during the colonies
Can be taken away, this is the reality.

Listen!
Your children will lead this nation
To tyranny or victory
To sin or purity
To God or Satan, the enemy.
This is the importance of a God-centered family.

My God is Great

Great is our Lord, and abundant in power;
his understanding is beyond measure.
Psalm 147:5

People question Your existence
But I see You in everything.
You have shown Your great strength
Through the power of hurricanes.
You have shown Your great majesty
Through the splendor of mighty mountains.
You've shown Your delicate hand
Through the details of a beautiful flower.

How then can I not exclaim:
My God is Great!
He is stronger than any hurricane,
He has more majesty and splendor
Than any mountain could ever have.
He is more beautiful than any delicate flower
Could ever be.

It strikes my heart to think
He took time to craft me in such detail,
That I am unique.
How can my knees not fall
In admiration, reverence, and fear
Of my Great Creator?

How can my lungs and voice not scream?
"Hallelujah, Amen, Glory to the King!"
I will not give my soul to the prince of the air
Only to the King of Kings.

Satan has no power over me!
When the devils are in Hell one day
I will be in Glory
Proclaiming forever God is Great because
My God was always Great!

The Wind

He caused the east wind to blow in the heavens,
and by his power he led out the south wind.
Psalm 78:6

As the wind passes over the sea
Our lives are like the breeze
It's here today and gone tomorrow
Without stopping
Even for a drink of tea.

You can hear it
When it wants to be heard,
You can feel it
When it wants to be felt,
You can see its effects
Upon the land and sea
And even in the trees.

Where does it come from?
Where does it go?
If it's like our lives
What becomes of our souls?
Do you know?
Trust in the One who does
Because He knows
Where the wind comes from
And Who created our souls!

Vanity

Vanity is like a cavity.
It starts small
But turns into agony.
It's something we desire
But soon will expire.
When death comes knocking at our door
The importance of vanity will be no more.
When we're in front of our Lord
All earthly things will fade away.
So leave it alone, push it aside,
Come to our Lord
For peace of heart and mind.

What Is Right?

Do not be conformed to this world, but be transformed by the renewal of your mind,
that by testing you may discern what is the will of God,
what is good and acceptable and perfect.

Romans 12:2

In this time of history
What is right and what is wrong?

The world says homosexuality is right
Because it's what they feel.
No, I say it's wrong
Because my heavenly Lord has told me so.

The world says abortion is right
Because it's a woman's right.
No, I say its murder.
To take away a life the Lord has given;
Only He can take what is His.

The world says divorce is right
Because it just didn't work out.
No, I say its adultery.
Who can separate what God Almighty
Has made into one.

The Word of God,
It tells us what is right and what is wrong,
What to do and not to do
To please His holy name.

Now you have to decide.
Are you going to stand with God's Word
And the truth of His ways?
Or
Are you going to listen and agree
To what the world and
The prince of the air have to say?

God is My Strength

I love you, O LORD, my strength. The LORD is my rock and my fortress and my deliverer, my God, my rock, in whom I take refuge, my shield, and the horn of my salvation, my stronghold. I call upon the LORD, who is worthy to be praised, and I am saved from my enemies.

Psalm 18:1-3

As I grow older in the faith
I realize the foolish things
I used to do day after day.

Thanks to Your Holy Spirit and Word
I am able to be corrected from that crooked path and follow
The straight way.

But there are moments
During the hurricane
That I feel You are far away.
Even though the eye of the storm
Has already passed,
I don't find any
Rest in the test.

Thanks be to You, my God,
Your Word never fails.
You are my rock, my stronghold, and strength.
For if You are with me, who can be against me?
No hurricanes, winds, or waves can move me!
Satan and his devils can't move me
For Jesus is my Rock for all eternity.

Where?

O LORD, you have searched me and known me!
You know when I sit down and when I rise up;
you discern my thoughts from afar.
You search out my path and my lying down
and are acquainted with all my ways.
Even before a word is on my tongue,
behold, O LORD, you know it altogether.
You hem me in, behind and before,
and lay your hand upon me.
Such knowledge is too wonderful for me;
it is high; I cannot attain it.
Where shall I go from your Spirit?
Or where shall I flee from your presence?
If I ascend to heaven, you are there!
If I make my bed in Sheol, you are there!

Psalm 139:1-8

Where can we hide?
From Your everlasting eye.

Where can we go?
Because You already know.

What can we say?
That you haven't heard before.

What can we do?
But believe in you!

Who Am I?

O LORD, our Lord, how majestic is your name in all the earth!
You have set your glory above the heavens.
Out of the mouth of babies and infants,
you have established strength because of your foes,
to still the enemy and the avenger.
When I look at your heavens, the work of your fingers,
the moon and the stars, which you have set in place,
what is man that you are mindful of him,
and the son of man that you care for him?

Psalm 8:1-4

As I read Your Holy Word everyday
My knees fall hard to the ground
In reverence and fear of Your Holy Name.
Jehovah, Yahweh, Adonai,
The King of Kings,
The Ruler of all the galaxies.

When I start to question You, God, in what You do
I stop immediately
And ask for forgiveness sincerely.
I ask myself,
"Where was I when You created the world?
When you gave instruction to the land and sea?"

You will have mercy on whom You will have mercy
And compassion on whom You will have compassion.
Who am I to question You in these things?
You are the One who can take away
The breath of life that You have given me.

Who am I?
That you would send Your Son
To die on the cross
For a worthless sinner such as I,
A worthless sinner such as I.

Which One Will You Be?

In this life you are one of two:
One who is righteous
Or one who is wicked;
One who is humble
Or one who is prideful;
One who is saved
Or one who is condemned.

Your wealth is worth nothing in the day of wrath,
Your own wickedness will bring you down.
All your hopes will perish with you in the lake of fire
When the King comes back again.

You are on one of two paths:
One that leads to glory
Or one that leads to Hell.

Are you saved in the blood of Christ?
Or are you condemned as the enemy of the living God?
Your life on earth is like the wind,
In the blink of an eye you could be standing before
The King of Kings, the Maker of all living things.
If you're not covered in the blood of Christ,
when the time comes
It'll be too late, it'll be too late.
You're either saved or condemned, there is no in-between
No matter what you may think. Which one will you be?

Christian Soldiers

Be strong in the Lord and in the strength of his might.
Put on the whole armor of God,
that you may be able to stand against the schemes of the devil.
For we do not wrestle against flesh and blood,
but against the rulers, against the authorities,
against the cosmic powers over this present darkness,
against the spiritual forces of evil in the heavenly places.
Ephesians 6:10-12

When has there ever been
A soldier sleeping on the battlefield?
For grievous indeed that would be.
But that is not the case for a true soldier of the King.
He knows about that slanderous snake
That creeps in the silence of darkness
And strikes to kill before you awake.

Sadly, there have been many to fall into the tempting slumber.
Wake up! Dear Christian soldiers,
For the enemy is at your door
And mercy is not a word in his vocabulary.

Where? Where, you may ask,
My dear Christian friend.
He is in disguise, of course.
Only the righteous in spirit
Can see past that cunning façade.

Wake up Christian soldiers!
For this is war
Not some festive party of sorts.
For the enemy will not think of stopping
Until the day the trumpets of the King
Start sounding.

Praise Be to You

Enter his gates with thanksgiving,
and his courts with praise!
Give thanks to him; bless his name!
For the LORD is good;
his steadfast love endures forever,
and his faithfulness to all generations.
Psalm 100:4-5

I come to You
On bended knee
By my sin that is before me.
I do not know
Why You would send Your Son below,
But I praise You with all my soul.

For if I had a son
I would not send him to the world below,
To walk the streets unknown,
To be virgin-born.
Who would have known?
Except for the shepherds in the fields, of course
Because we all know how the story goes.

For I would have sent him on a chariot of fire
In such glorious attire
There would be no doubt he was the Messiah.

Praise be to You,
My heavenly King!
From a babe to a cross
You made it to be,
To save a soul
So worthless and unclean.
Praise be to Jesus Christ
Son of the King.

To The Lost

*Let it be known to all of you and to all the people of Israel
that by the name of Jesus Christ of Nazareth,
whom you crucified, whom God raised from the dead
—by him this man is standing before you well.
This Jesus is the stone that was rejected by you,
the builders, which has become the cornerstone.
And there is salvation in no one else,
for there is no other name under heaven
given among men by which we must be saved."*

Acts 4:10-12

We are made from the dust
But do not praise Him who is greater than us.
We entertain the lies of Satan
Instead of looking for redemption.
We look for riches
That will surely vanish.
We want the world
Instead of the Word.
When you are before Him
Don't say you never knew.

For the saved, we are at ease,
For we are washed in the blood
Of our Redeemer.
It's in the Holy Word He sent us.
Didn't you read that He came
So the lost would be found and
To forgive us of our evil ways?

To the lost,
Now is the time
To come to the feet of Him
Who died on the cross
As the selfless, perfect lamb.
His name is Jesus Christ,
The Holy Lamb!